BELIEVE
AND
GROW SMART

7 Fun, Easy-to-Follow, Classroom Tested, Reading Strategies to Help Your Child Improve Over a Grade Level in Reading

NOEL MORALES, M.ED.

Connect the Dots Learning, LLC
210 N. Malden Ave.
Fullerton, CA. 92832
www.BelieveAndGrowSmart.com

Ordering Information:
Quantity sales. Special discounts are available on quantity purchases by school districts, non-profit organizations, and others. For details, contact the publisher at the address above or at info@connectthedotslearning.com

To all parents, grandparents, aunts, uncles, brothers, sisters, General Education Teachers, Special Education Teachers, Speech and Language Pathologists, Occupational Therapists, Psychologists, Administrators, support staff, advocates and all the countless others who I've inadvertently failed to mention… who work tirelessly to improve the psychological, social, emotional and academic well-being of children that struggle to read.

And to my wife Mami who supports and encourages me always.

Thank you.

CONTENTS

ACKNOWLEDGMENTS

I HAVE BEEN TRULY BLESSED to have had many encouraging supportive people in my life, without who's help I would not have gained the knowledge and personal experiences to have finished this book. I love going to work every day and spending time with all the talented children and their families. As anyone who has written a book knows, it takes a lot of time, but with the right support systems it's a bit easier. I want to thank everyone who helped me get this book done. I'd be remiss to think that I can thank everyone who helped here, but since I get a page to try, I'll mention a few.

An enormous thanks to all of my mentors I've had since 1997. Thanks to James Messrah, Mercedes Santoyo, Robert Samples, Janet Montoya, Claudine Ajeti, Clif de Cordoba and Celia R. Dominguez. Without you I would have never become the teacher I am now.

I want to especially thank all of the thousands of teachers, students, parents and clients that I have had the remarkable pleasure of serving for nearly two decades. I have learned from all of them and every encounter brought me lessons for much of what I am sharing in this book. Thank You!

Also, I want to thank my grandma and grandpa for having the most amazing kindness and belief in me. Grandpa… a huge hug to you who I miss so much. Thank you to my mom; my sisters Birdiee and April; and my brother Stuart.

Finally, a very special thanks to my wife Mami, the love of my life, and without who's help I could not do most of what I do. Thank you for being there for me, keeping me grounded and for inspiring me at the same time!

INTRODUCTION

Dear Friend, Welcome to Believe and Grow Smart. This represents 18 years of hard work, experience and the efforts of my incredible team, students and their families I've served under many capacities, teachers I've supported and clients. Maybe you're one of them!

Usually, clients come to me to seek help because their children are behind in one or more subject areas and they need help now. Their children have run into personal challenges at a very young age about their beliefs. They have run into limiting beliefs and have created obstacles in their own minds that they feel are insurmountable. They have recurring thoughts in their mind that they are dumb. That they can't read. That they aren't good at math. Most of these thoughts are continuously playing in their minds all day long in school and have a significant impact on their learning.

Let me ask you some questions that I ask my clients. If you could find a way to help your children build their academic self-confidence right now, this month, would you do it? How about improving their reading ability? Math ability? Writing ability? Maybe improving their reading, writing or math skills a grade level plus?

Yes, yes, yes, yes and yes. Right? I mean of course. Who wouldn't want their child to improve?

I'm here to tell you that it is not only possible to do exactly that, but that it definitely will happen if you are committed to your child's progress. I am not boasting or bragging. I've been a part of helping thousands of students and their families in grades K-12, Special Education and adults who returned to school to work on the General Education Development (GED) test, High School Diploma or to better their lives and the lives of their families by learning English. As you can see these students and their families comprise different ages and backgrounds. Families just like yours and students just like your children.

The ideas, principles and strategies of this book are designed to help you leverage my experience and know how. To help your children (possibly you too) expand and challenge their beliefs and allow them to have a brighter and fuller future. I want to tell you now that a single idea, when it is part of our beliefs, will change the course of life from the moment it is accepted. Doors are opened or closed. Futures are defined or lost.

Be very clear about this: I am not here to solve everything. I'm here to guide you so that you can help your children improve. I am here to help you raise the bar for them in a genuine, caring and compassionate manner. I am here to help them raise the bar for themselves and to extinguish the limiting beliefs that they have erroneously instilled in their minds.

Allow me to pause for a second and take a moment to share some thoughts with you in no particular order about what to expect in this book.

First, it's not passive. On the contrary, it's interactive. You will have many opportunities for you to go deeper in the content, gain access to several free training videos, participate in some interactive webinar events and register to get my up-to-date trainings.

Second, this book is intended for parents that WILL take action and not let one more day go by where their children are struggling to read. You'll see there's LOTS of ideas that you can use to help children gain confidence and reach their potential. If you're the type who's looking for a free, quick, effortless and easy way, this isn't the book for you. I'm not here to lie to you.

Third, this book is intended and designed to start a conversation with you, give us a chance to get to know each other better, develop trust, a bond and ultimately help us decide if we should work together someday.

Fourth, this is a book that's packed with content and lots of ideas. It's a WHAT book. My intention for you and the purpose of this book is to show you the most powerful ways and teaching strategies that can help your child improve, regain their academic self-confidence and to build resiliency and grit that they can translate into other areas of their lives. We have a how to system available that includes everything you need to execute what you read in these pages.

I want to help your children maximize their potential and add value to your life. You'll notice that there are opportunities throughout this book to register and watch videos and YES, I do have some great products I'd like to sell to you because they work and you'll have a better life and relationship with your children.

If you like what you read, or most of what you read, I'd absolutely, positively love to hear from you and get to know you better and find out what you learned - or better yet, post a picture or video on the Connect the Dots Learning Facebook wall at www.Facebook.com/ConnectTheDotsLearning.

The BEST way to start a relationship with me will be to visit the web link below, watch the free training videos, post your comments on the comment wall and I'll see it and do my best to respond to you. I'm looking forward to getting to know you better!

FREE BOOK UPDATES AND VIDEO TRAINING

This book is INTERACTIVE - to get free training videos, access to more resources and updates and first-hand knowledge when our hybrid math workbooks are released,

visit www.BelieveAndGrowSmart.com **or text GROWSMART to 58885 or text your email address to (844) 906-0506 or scan this fancy QR code**

1 THE MOST SUCCESSFUL STRATEGIES

> *"We all have dreams.*
> *But in order to make dreams come into reality,*
> *it takes an awful lot of determination,*
> *dedication, self-discipline, and effort".*
> Jesse Owens

Dear friend, I want to thank you for taking the time to read this book and allowing me to share with you the most effective reading strategies to help your child succeed in school. My personal mission is to help all children nationwide reach their maximum potential and unleash the academic power that they have within. I am pleased to say that my team and I at Connect the Dots Learning have helped all children improve in the areas that they have had struggles in. This is great news for you because the tantrums will go away, the battles of getting their homework done will get eliminated, your child's frustration will minimize, your frustration will be reduced, their behavior will improve and you will have more time to enjoy your child be a child. My goal for you as well is to give you back more time, freedom and happiness.

And I'll show you irrefutable proof via case studies that these strategies and methods work for any child in any grade that is struggling to read. You may think you've heard this before or maybe you have even already gotten tutors or taken them to expensive learning centers, but my guess is your child may not be performing as well as you or they would like to. It's okay… and it's not your fault.

What you're about to experience is a *new way to think*, so hang on. You're about to discover a completely different way to help your child improve in reading…and you're also about to see how quickly your child can achieve stellar results…the results you want.

You're going to meet several of my students and their families from all walks of life, ages and socioeconomic status in these pages and you'll have a chance to watch several bonus videos that will walk you through the process too.

In this chapter, you'll learn the three fatal misconceptions you've been led to believe about your child catching up; and, even better, I'll show you a simple system that you or anyone can use to overcome these challenges.

Now, if you haven't registered already, make sure you sign up to get the bonus videos—**the link is at the end of this chapter.** They're educational and entertaining, packed with tips, ideas and strategies you can use right now to help your child succeed. It's a gift from me to you.

Please don't confuse my excitement with hype—I'm just so excited for you to be holding this book and learning these secrets. My goal for you is to show you a system, up until now, only a few people implement…and it works like crazy.

So, who am I and why should you listen to me? If you don't know my story, I'm NOT a Harvard graduate. In fact, I'm a product of Special Education myself.

I was born in Managua Nicaragua. My family and I left a politically torn country in the midst of a civil war and immigrated to the United States in 1980. I never met my biological father. I did not know how to speak English. I did not have health insurance as a child. I grew up with my grandparents and my uncle in a tiny two bedroom apartment in Korea town; a densely populated area in Los Angeles California. But all the while, I was blessed.

My story begins with me hating to speak and read... I was a fourth grader in Mrs. Kapitz' class. I remember working so hard on my book report and presentation for my class. As children were being chosen to present, I began to get nervous and anxious. This is where it all began and this is why I care so much about children that struggle in school.

I went up and I had the book in my hand. I began to speak and I began to stutter immediately. My classmates began to laugh. But wait, I am not a quitter. So I continued even though I felt horrible. The more I spoke, the more I stuttered. The more I stuttered the more the children laughed at me. I can't express to you enough how horrible I felt. I felt different, I felt stupid, I felt worthless.

This feeling was to endure for the next 15 plus years of my life. Every time I was in class throughout my primary education, secondary education, post-secondary education and graduate school I felt dumb even though I was smart.

During language arts time in elementary school all I would think about was the teacher not picking me to read. In my mind all I would say, over and over again was "please don't pick me to read, please don't pick me to read, please don't pick me to read." When I was in my English classes or my Social Studies or History classes in Junior High or High School all I would think about was "please don't pick me to read, please don't pick me to read, please don't pick me to read." I'll be honest, I could not

3

concentrate on the subject matter. I had to work harder at home so that I could keep up with all of my classes.

I attended the University of California Irvine and the same issues appeared but not to the same degree. The professors lecturing to us in the large lecture halls of 500 plus students did help me. I didn't have to read out loud anymore! But I lacked self-confidence and had low self-esteem whenever I spoke. I didn't pursue friendships because I was embarrassed about my speech impediment. But that was not what hurt the most. What hurt me the most was that I wanted to become an attorney but I recall visualizing myself in a court room trying to defend my client or cross examining a witness and saying, "I o-o-o-o-o-b-b-b-j-j-ject! Your honor." I can still to this day visualize this picture in my mind because I attached so much meaning to it. What hurt the most was that I did not pursue my dream because I thought I could not do it. This is why I especially care about children that struggle in school because I don't want them to have any limitations to their dreams.

I firmly believe that with the right supports, strategies, determination and a burning desire to achieve their goals they are certainly attainable. This is my life mission and my calling. This is what I love to do. I have felt what your child is feeling now. I have felt dumb. I have felt different. I did not like to read. I have first-hand experience knowing what it feels like to want to but feeling defeated and believing that it's impossible.

But the good news is that I am here to help. By implementing the strategies that I have learned over the course of nearly two decades my team and I have helped thousands of children and their families.

One of my favorite success stories is E.S., who I battled fiercely to keep in general education. He thrived in my class and continued to be in a general education environment. Another is R.R., an eighth grader that was performing at a mid-third grade level. In just three months of one on one intensive instruction, I was able to unlock his true potential and confidence and he grew three academic grade levels!

Now the great news is, I actually did not become an attorney . I'm here with you today as an educator! It's really nice to be doing what I love to do and making an impact on the lives of children that need it the most on a daily basis. I beat my own limiting beliefs, which means I can continue on my personal life mission of helping 1,000,000 children and families!

After working with so many students and families we've found that most make three fatal mistakes which prevent their children from either improving altogether or making the strides that they can make.

The first mistake is called the "Lazy Assumption". That's thinking that your child is lazy. I don't consider myself lazy, but ask me to do something I'm horrible at and all of a sudden I will find every reason and every excuse not to do it. Does that mean I am lazy? Not necessarily. It just means that the activity or task I am asked to do gives me more pain than pleasure. Think about something you feel you're not very good at. How would you react? Now ask yourself, is that being lazy? Probably not.

Mistake number two is something we call the "It's going to get better syndrome." That's thinking that if you put in a minimal amount of effort and just let the school deal with your child's difficulties that they will improve. Many of our students and their families didn't sit passively waiting for things to improve. They took it upon themselves to be proactive and get their children the help that they needed before the problem escalated. They didn't start out feeling confident either. But they took a chance… and took action with our proven system… and now, their children are making the strides that they deserve. Don't you want the same thing?

Mistake number three is conveniently named after one of the biggest companies in the world. It's called "Walmart BS." That's believing and thinking that you have to go to a national tutoring franchise to get results. It's just not true —many of our students and families have gone to national tutoring franchises and have been dismally disappointed .

Throughout the book, I will give you strategies that work that you can implement at home right now. I will also share with you several students that my team and I have helped. Children just like yours. These will be noted as case studies. To protect the privacy of the children and their families they will be referred as case study 1, case study 2 and so forth. Let's get started! To your child's success!

LET'S BE PROACTIVE!

Do you like what you've read so far? Well, how about watching, listening and interacting! There are some cool training videos and step-by-step exercises **visit** www.BelieveAndGrowSmart.com **or text**

GROWSMART to 58885 or text your email address to (844) 906-0506

---

2 BUILD YOUR CHILD'S SELF-CONFIDENCE

"One of the greatest discoveries a man makes, one of his great surprises, is to find he can do what he was afraid he couldn't do."
Henry Ford

I want to tell you right now that everything else in this book will not matter if your child does not have the resilience, the grit and the perseverance to be able to tackle obstacles that face him/her. This chapter is very near and dear to me. This is just not something that I believe in, it is something that has made an impact on my life and has the possibility of making a profound impact on your child's life too. This involves building their self-confidence.

Children have to understand that it's okay to make a mistake. I know that parents and teachers usually tell children not to be afraid to ask questions. They tell them "don't be afraid to make mistakes". But then they are not always congruent about what they say. Let me explain to you what that means. There are also times that we tell children that there are no dumb questions, that it's okay to ask questions. But when children or even adults for that matter ask questions that may seem easy for us, we don't give off that real and genuine sense of "it's okay to ask this question". "It's okay if you don't understand". Sometimes we give off the impression of… "really? You're asking that question? You don't know that?"

I really want to stress that it's truly important that we always encourage children to do things even if they are difficult. And that it's okay if they make mistakes, it's okay if they don't understand, it's okay if things need to be clarified once, twice, three or even ten times. The goal is for them to be able to understand it. Once they know that: "it's okay to make a mistake, it's okay to not understand a concept immediately, but they *WILL* eventually get it", they are going to have a completely different attitude. They will begin to build resilience which will help them overcome not just academic obstacles, but obstacles in general. We must instill in them a never quit attitude. It's okay to fail, it's okay to make mistakes because at some point they are going to get it.

Parents, I need you to know from the outset that we have to exert constant outstanding effort and have to realize that things will not always be super easy. We have to realize that challenges and obstacles will come our way. But we also have to realize that we're going to do it. That we're going to get it. That we have the belief that we are going to get it. But more importantly, we have to know what our goal is and have a burning desire to get it because our goal *IS* attainable. When we struggle we should never look at it as a failure, we need to see things as they are, but not worse than they are. We just say to ourselves "okay, I tried this it didn't work, so I just need to try something else". Often times it's just a matter of tweaking it a little bit in order to get the desired outcome. I can't guarantee you that after the 2nd time or the 10th time or the 150th time they are going to get it. But eventually one will find the formula that will create success. Little things do make a difference.

feel confident recognizing the words.

So here is the last round. The last piece is for you to put the flashcards on the table or desk in front of them and have them show you what the words are and this time they will read the sentence on the back. So you will say, show me the word "this". They will pick up the flashcard. Ask them to turn it over and read you the sentence. They will say (and you can help them), "This is my favorite game." Great! Next say, "show me the word are." They will pick up the flashcard and show you the word "are". Ask them to turn it over and read the sentence to you. They will say, " Are you going to take me to the park?" Awesome! Next say, "show me the word the." They will pick up the flashcard. Ask them to turn it over and read you the sentence. They will say, " The dog is barking at the cat." Wonderful! Finally say, "show me the word one." They will pick up the flashcard. Ask them to turn it over and read the sentence to you. They will say, " I have one kitten." Fantastic! Repeat this process at least twice so that you build their confidence in their ability to read these sight words.

I want you to add new sight words as often as possible (preferably daily). Now that you know the process make sure to utilize this strategy so that they can build their sight word vocabulary. Remember to review the words that they have previously been exposed to on a daily basis so that they can truly recall them. One of the great things about doing this activity is that as they learn sight words and read sentences that they generated using their own words, they will see other sight words appear which will reinforce their sight word recognition even more!

Below is a *sample* list of fourth grade sight words that you may wish to use with your child to practice this strategy.

Fourth Grade Sight Words

action

actually

addition

Africa

aim

American

angle

area

art

battle

being

between

breakfast

capital

caught

center

century

check

circle

clothes

colony

compare

compound

contain

copy

cried

current

demand

design

dictionary

difficult

distance

drawing

elect

element

entire

equation

exactly

experiment

express

famous

fear

flow

forest

general

grown

hadn't

heat

height

hospital

huge

increase

industry

interesting

knew

least

level

loud

lying

measure

melody

million

modern

music

national

neighbor

noise

nothing

numeral

opposite

oxygen

pattern

perhaps

planet

police

possible

problem

produce

provide

pupil

raise

region

represent

rhythm

scientist

segment

sentence

several

short

simple

sincerely

solve

special

spent

statement

stone

subject

sudden

supply

surface

system

term

though

tomorrow

travel

tube

underline

value

voice

wasn't

within

written

CASE STUDY 6 (Initial Assessment)

Gender: male

Grade: 3.7

Age: 8 years, 6 months

Reading Test Results

Word Identification:	GE 2.2	AE 7-7
Reading Fluency:	GE 2.5	AE 7-10
Story Recall:	GE 1.5	AE 6-10
Understanding Directions:	GE K.7	AE 6-6
Passage Comprehension:	GE 2.4	AE 7-9
Word Attack:	GE 1.9	AE 7-5
Oral Comprehension:	GE 3.0	AE 8-8
Reading Vocabulary:	GE 2.8	AE 8-5
Sound Awareness:	GE 1.3	AE 6-8

I got a call from a father that wanted to get help for his son that was underperforming in language arts. Prior to the initial consultation I asked him to bring any supporting documents such as his report card or work samples so that I could get a better understanding of what his needs were.

When I met with the father he told me that his son was not very motivated to read. He also indicated that he would become easily distracted and would need multiple reminders to get his homework done. He was concerned on two fronts: 1) his reading ability and 2) his attention and concentration. I asked him if the school had any concerns about his son's progress and attention and he said no that his teacher would say that he's a little behind but it wasn't a major cause for concern.

Let's talk about the results of the test. The areas of relative strength were in reading vocabulary and oral comprehension. The areas that needed attention and support were his ability to use phonics and decoding as well as word attack skills, reading fluency and comprehension. With respect to the father's concern about his son's attention, I did not observe an inability to focus or concentrate on the part of his son during the testing session.

The manner in which I designed the plan of attack was to address his word attack skills by strengthening his phonics and decoding skills and building on his reading fluency. I knew that the comprehension would follow because he did fairly well on the oral comprehension subtest. I worked with him for 40 hours on a one on one basis during the course of 5 months. Below are the results of the post-assessment.

CASE STUDY 6 (Post-Assessment)

Gender: male

Grade: 4.0

Age: 8 years, 11 months

Reading Test Results

Word Identification:	GE 3.1	AE 8-5
Reading Fluency:	GE 3.2	AE 8-8
Story Recall:	GE 2.4	AE 7-11
Understanding Directions:	GE 2.6	AE 8-2
Passage Comprehension:	GE 3.4	AE 8-8
Word Attack:	GE 2.7	AE 8-3
Oral Comprehension:	GE 3.9	AE 9-8
Reading Vocabulary:	GE 3.8	AE 9-2
Sound Awareness:	GE 2.6	AE 8-2

I was so proud of this young man. He worked super hard and made outstanding progress. During the time that I worked with him I paid close attention to see if he had any concentration or attention issues. I never saw him exhibit behaviors that would elicit a red flag. He was a model student. During the course of four months he was able to improve over an entire grade level in the areas that he needed support. What a wonderful outcome. It is such a joy to see children become more confident with their reading ability while enjoying the process.

The formula and the recipe consists of the following: 1) getting children to believe in themselves that they CAN do it; 2) getting their parents to understand that they are not lazy and to provide them with as much support and positive reinforcement; and 3) implementing an academic program that is specific to them and their needs so that they can succeed and make progress as quickly as possible.

I LOVE MY CLIENTS!

I'd like to meet you and potentially develop a relationship with you so that I can be of service. Follow my Google+ page at http://www.plus.google.com/ConnectTheDotsLearning. Don't forget to get your free videos **visit** www.BelieveAndGrowSmart.com **or text GROWSMART to 58885 or text your email address to (844) 906-0506**

8 STRATEGY 4: CHUNKING

> *"An education isn't how much you have committed to memory,*
> *or even how much you know.*
> *It's being able to differentiate between what you know and what you don't."*
> *Anatole France*

Let's talk about the next strategy which is called chunking. Chunking requires using memory strategies therefore I will talk about some basic concepts of memory for a brief moment. Our human memory consists of these three basic memories. They are:

- sensory store
- short-term store
- long-term store

Sensory store is the oldest and quickest type of memory that we have. We have two sensory memory systems: 1) iconic memory (visual memory) and 2) echoic memory (auditory memory). At any given moment there are thousands of stimuli all around us. Because there are thousands of stimuli that we are encountered with, we have to pick out which ones will have any meaning to us. In essence, we quickly sift and sort through all of this stimuli to see what our brain will process. Imagine if our brain was able to process the thousands and thousands of stimuli entering our brain all at once? We wouldn't be able to handle it. We would have sensory overload.

The next memory is called short-term store or short-term memory. Once we have an input come in through or sensory memory; whether it be visual or auditory, our short term memory decides right away whether the information will be meaningful or not. It determines quickly whether it's important for you to remember the information or if it will just fade away.

Finally, we have a memory called long-term store or long-term memory. When trying to remember anything, the goal is to attach meaning to it so that it has an opportunity to be stored into our long-term memory. We want to remember things for the long haul. We don't want children to study for a test and then the next week forget what they studied so hard for. I'm sure that you have had this experience a least several times during the course of your life. You study for some time and then you do well on a test to later forget what you studied. This happens to all of us. The goal that we have at Connect the Dots Learning is to have children attach meaning to what they are learning so that they can remember what they've learned, internalize it, and have the ability to recall it. So let's talk about chunking.

Chunking is the ability to get large pieces of information and break it down to less components so that it is more manageable. Therefore, if we have ten numbers and if we were able to break it down to three or four more manageable pieces we would increase our chances of recalling those numbers. Note, our memory has the ability to store 7 ± 2 items at once (the range is 5-9 items). That means that for the average person s/he will be able to recall between 5-9 items. However, the smaller number of items one has to remember, the better chances one will remember.

Let's talk about a couple of examples that everyone is familiar with. Does this pattern look familiar? 123-45-6789. What about this pattern? (555) 123-4567.

The first example noted above that utilizes the chunking strategy are social security numbers. There are a total of nine digits in our social security number but instead of having to remember nine isolated numbers we have them chunked into three manageable pieces. The next example noted above that uses chunking are phone numbers. Instead of having to remember ten isolated digits, again we have them broken up into three comprehensible chunks. What's easier to remember nine or ten numbers or three chunks? So how do we apply this to reading?

When we are teaching children how to read especially as they progress into second grade and above, we want to explicitly teach children how to chunk multi-syllable words. Do you recall the chapter that went over the color coding strategy? Great! The color coding strategy when used to learn multi-syllable words is also utilizing the chunking strategy.

So let's go over a few words together. The first one is *chunking*. Chunking has two syllables, chunk-ing. Again, have your child color code the word like this, chunk**ing** or break up the word like this while continuing to use the color coding strategy chunk-**ing**. This makes reading and spelling easier. How do you spell chunking? /ch//u//n//k/ chunk and /ing/ ing, chunking. Children will begin to see a pattern such as the "ing" pattern when reading new words and when attempting to spell new words such as talk**ing**, play**ing**, think**ing**, sing**ing**, jump**ing** etc. Another example is the word *information*. Information can be chunked in the following manner: in-**for**-*ma*-**tion** or info**r***ma***tion**. The word information can look intimidating to a young reader because there are eleven letters in the word. However, when broken up into parts you can say, you know the part in. You know the part for. The next part is mā. Finally, the last part "tion" is

/shun/. Therefore the word is information. This becomes a lot easier to handle. Again, they will begin to recognize word parts and patterns. Therefore, when they encounter words with "tion" they will know that it is read /shun/ like competi**tion**, accusa**tion**, inspira**tion** and connec**tion**. The last example that I want to go over with you is the word masticate, which means to chew. Masticate can be chunked like this mas-**tic**-*ate* or mas**tic***ate*. The word masticate has been broken down into three syllables. This is a lot easier than trying to sound out nine individual letters.

I hope that this strategy is clear to you, why we use it and why it has proven to be an effective strategy. I assure you that the more consistent you are using this strategy, the more you practice this technique with your child, the more progress you will see.

Here is a sample list of third grade "must know" words that you can practice the chunking strategy with your child.

Third Grade Must-Know Words

address

adverb

annual

area

author

awhile

beggar

belong

bookshelf

buffalo

calendar

captain

castle

ceiling

cheating

cheerful

climate

clover

congruent

contest

cradle

cylinder

darling

delicious

deserve

direction

disappear

discussion

division

donkey

double

eagle

earliest

electricity

energetic

enjoyable

equivalent

escape

explore

factory

factual

feather

foreign

forgetful

furniture

gasoline

government

graduate

harmful

horseback

improve

include

interesting

invitation

junior

kettle

language

listen

lumber

machine

marble

mathematics

mayor

measurement

mention

millimeter

million

multiplication

national

newspaper

officer

oyster

paragraph

passenger

patient

photo

pollution

potatoes

product

puzzle

receive

refrigerator

report

ridiculous

safety

scissors

settle

signal

similarity

sprinkle

squirrel

subtraction

symmetry

temperature

tomato

truthful

ugliest

vacation

CASE STUDY 7 (Initial Assessment)

Gender: female

Grade: 3.9

Age: 9 years, 4 months

Reading Test Results

Word Identification:	GE 2.2	AE 7-7
Reading Fluency:	GE 2.4	AE 7-9
Story Recall:	GE 2.5	AE 8-0
Understanding Directions:	GE 3.3	AE 8-9
Passage Comprehension:	GE 1.7	AE 7-0
Word Attack:	GE 1.9	AE 7-5
Oral Comprehension:	GE 3.0	AE 8-8
Reading Vocabulary:	GE 2.7	AE 8-4
Sound Awareness:	GE 1.5	AE 6-11

I got a call from a mother that wanted to get help for her daughter that was having a difficult time reading. Prior to the initial consultation I asked her to bring her report card and assessments so that I could see how she was performing in class.

I had the pleasure of meeting with both the mother and father. The mother communicated to me that ever since her daughter was in kindergarten she saw that she was having struggles. She told me that she would express her concerns with her teachers but they would always say that she would grow out of it. The father mentioned to me that ever since first grade they obtained outside help for their daughter. They hired a teacher to work with her at their house. That didn't help. They also enrolled her at a tutoring center that is well known nationwide. That also didn't help. They tried to get help at her school but the teachers would continually tell the family that they did not see any major concerns. The mother went on to say that she was still confused when she would write the letters "b" and "d". Remember that their daughter was in late third grade at the time. If this were true, then I am not sure why the teachers that she previously had and her current teacher did not express concern about this child's reading. I agree that if kindergarten or even a first grade student is still mixing up the letters "b" and "d" that it is still within the normal range of development. However, a third grader? This was of concern to me.

Her parents were also wondering if she was just being lazy. I responded that if she was still reversing letters and still having a difficult time reading even with all of the outside intervention that they had obtained for her , that the chances were that she wasn't lazy. I also reminded the mother that because she had concerns about her daughter's reading since kindergarten, that she most likely was struggling to read.

Let's talk about the results of the test. The areas of relative strength were in reading vocabulary and oral comprehension. The areas that needed attention and support were her ability to use phonics & decoding as well as word attack skills, reading fluency and reading comprehension. When I was done testing her, I was highly concerned because she was about two grade levels behind in reading. During testing, I make sure to observe children when they read and how they perform on the tasks. As I observed her, I noticed that she would not use decoding strategies. Furthermore, I observed her skipping words, reading words out of order and she would skip lines when reading. I suggested that her parents request from the school that she get tested to see if she qualified for Special Education services.

I knew I could help her improve but I was also realistic. I knew that it wouldn't be easy. I was going to have to make the material fun and

the time to read this story over the course of a week and you will see that every day they will become more and more comfortable reading the story on their own. I really want you to give them multiple opportunities to practice one story. Remember, we want them to build their confidence. Let's look at the eighth case study.

CASE STUDY 8 (Initial Assessment)

Gender: male

Grade: 2.6

Age: 8 years, 3 months

Reading Test Results

Word Identification:	GE K.6	AE 5-11
Reading Fluency:	GE <K.0	AE <4-1
Story Recall:	GE 1.7	AE 7-0
Understanding Directions:	GE 1.5	AE 6-10
Passage Comprehension:	GE K.5	AE 5-9
Word Attack:	GE K.3	AE 5-7
Oral Comprehension:	GE 3.0	AE 8-4
Reading Vocabulary:	GE <K.7	AE <6-0
Sound Awareness:	GE <K.0	AE 4-5

I got a call from a mother that wanted to get help for her son that was having an extremely difficult time reading. Prior to the initial consultation I asked her to bring his Individualized Education Program (IEP), report card and assessments so that I could see what supports he needed to begin to make improvements.

I met with the mother during the initial consultation. She indicated to me that he had a bad experience with school in first grade. He was so behind that he would misbehave in class and would not cooperate with the teacher. He was assessed for Special Education in first grade and was eligible for Special Education services under a Specific Learning Disability (SLD). He was also diagnosed with Attention Deficit Hyperactivity Disorder (ADHD). Furthermore, he was receiving Language and Speech services. Her son was placed in a Special Day Class (SDC) so that his educational needs were met. When she communicated to me all of this information, I knew that he was significantly behind but I wasn't sure how much he was behind. The mother hired a retired teacher to work with him but he did not respond to her at all. In fact, he did not benefit from the private tutoring per the mother

The mother was also concerned about her son shutting down when asked to read. She mentioned to me that he would not try or make any attempts to read independently. Furthermore, that he had trouble retaining and recalling what he previously had learned.

Let's talk about the results of the test. The area of strength for this young man was in oral comprehension. In fact, he was above grade level in this area. However, he needed tremendous amounts of support in all of the other areas of reading. I wanted to see how he performed when recognizing lower and uppercase letters and what initial vowel sounds and consonant sounds he knew. He demonstrated that he knew 18 uppercase letters, 12 lowercase letters and 9 sounds. He was already over 2 grade levels behind and needed quick intervention. He was working at a mid-Kindergarten level.

The areas that needed attention and support were his ability to recognize letters and sounds, phonics & decoding strategies, reading fluency and reading comprehension. I designed a program specifically tailored to his needs and interests. The plan of attack was for him to master letter recognition, phonemic awareness and sound-symbol relationships. I worked with him for 16 hours on a one on one basis during the course of 2 months. Below are the results of the post-assessment.

CASE STUDY 8 (Post-Assessment)

Gender: male

Grade: 2.8

Age: 8 years, 5 months

Reading Test Results

Word Identification:	GE K.9	AE 6-2
Reading Fluency:	GE<K .7	AE <5-10
Story Recall:	GE 3.3	AE 8-9
Understanding Directions:	GE 2.2	AE 7-6
Passage Comprehension:	GE K.9	AE 6-2
Word Attack:	GE K.8	AE 6-1
Oral Comprehension:	GE 3.3	AE 8-11
Reading Vocabulary:	GE K.8	AE 6-0
Sound Awareness:	GE K.6	AE 6-0

This young man made outstanding progress during the 16 hours that I worked with him on a one on one basis. He learned all of the letters or the alphabet as well as the initial consonant sounds and short vowel sounds. He also learned 32 sight words! Furthermore, he felt more comfortable decoding consonant-vowel-consonant (CVC) words. His phonemic awareness skills improved dramatically. In fact, he received an award at school because he had shown so much progress! Don't get me wrong, he still needs an extensive amount of support and has a long way to go, but he has regained his confidence and ability to read. Not just that, he is trying harder and wants to get better!

The formula and the recipe consists of the following: 1) getting children to believe in themselves that they CAN do it; 2) getting their parents to understand that they are not lazy and to provide them with as much support and positive reinforcement; and 3) implementing an academic program that is specific to them and their needs so that they can succeed and make progress as quickly as possible

---

CONVERSATION EXERCISE

There's a step-by-step video exercise that guides you through coming up with a great way to talk to your child to uncover the struggles that s/he may be having to read. You also have an opportunity to have a records review with me and see if we can determine what types of support(s) your child might need.

Visit www.BelieveAndGrowSmart.com **or text GROWSMART to 58885 or text your email address to (844) 906-0506**

Response strategy is for children to internalize the meaning and to truly learn the word utilizing their kinesthetic memory. Let's take a look at the next word.

Fire Extinguisher

This is what I would say. "You may not want to become a firefighter when you grow up, but you know what a firefighter does right? They ride around in the huge red fire trucks and they put out fires." The child will say "yes". Then I will say, "Let's pretend that you're a firefighter. You have on your firefighter gear, you get a call. You go down the firefighter pole at the fire station. You get into the fire truck with the other firefighters. Then you drive out of the station and go to the location where the fire is at, so you can put out the fire. So you get to the location where the fire is at. You notice that it's not a big fire. So what you do, is you'll get the big red fire extinguisher from the wall and you will start to extinguish the fire with the fire extinguisher." Note: I am showing them the Total Physical Response and demonstrating the movements and the sound of the fire extinguisher while I am putting out the small fire. They are looking at me attentively. Then I will say, "Okay. Let's do it together. You're at the fire station. You get a call that there is a fire nearby. You put on your firefighter gear. You go down the pole at the fire station. You get in the fire truck with the other firefighters. You arrive at the location. You notice that it's not an enormous fire. So you reach to the wall and get the red fire extinguisher. Go ahead and extinguish the fire. Make the sound that the fire extinguisher would make. SHHHHHHHHHHHHHHH. Great!" Now I will ask them to show me "fire extinguisher". They will grab the fire extinguisher from the wall and make the sound that a fire extinguisher would make while in use. Again, they would learn this word by tapping into their kinesthetic memory. Let's look at the last example.

Elated

So now let's do the last word, elated. I would say, "Imagine that it's your tenth birthday. Your parents are going to take you to Disneyland. But guess what? They are also going to take you to Magic Mountain. But wait, they are also going to take you to the toy store and you can pick anything form the store. But it has to be one thing. But wait! Afterwards you're going to have an awesome birthday party at your house and you get to invite all of your friends! Is that cool or what? How would you feel?" The child would say, "I would feel happy! I would feel excited! That would be awesome!" Then I would say, "Exactly. That is what elated means. So when you are elated you are jumping for joy because you are so excited. So when I say elated, I want you to imagine that your parents told you that they're going to take you to Disneyland and Magic Mountain. They will take you to a toy store and you can pick out anything you want. Plus, you will have an enormous birthday party at your house and you will get to invite all of your friends. So when I say show me elated, I want you to jump as high as you can and say YAY as loud as you can." Remember, as you are talking to them I want you to show them the movements. Paint a clear picture in their mind. So now I would say, "show me elated." The child would jump up high in the air and say "YAY!"

To conclude this exercise I would tell them, "show me masticate. Show me fire extinguisher. Show me elated." They would do the Total Physical Response to demonstrate the meaning of the word. I would continue to ask them, "show me fire extinguisher. Show me elated. Show

Story Recall:	GE 5.9	AE 11-2
Understanding Directions:	GE 3.7	AE 9-1
Passage Comprehension:	GE 2.9	AE 8-3
Word Attack:	GE 3.9	AE 9-2
Oral Comprehension:	GE 3.5	AE 9-2
Reading Vocabulary:	GE 3.8	AE 9-2
Sound Awareness:	GE 2.6	AE 8-2

This young lady made outstanding progress during the 36 hours that I worked with her on a one on one basis. She demonstrated that she enjoyed reading, but needed some help with word attack strategies. Her reading fluency improved and her comprehension improved as a result of focusing on meaning rather on trying to read individual words. Overall, she improved approximately seven months worth of school!

The formula and the recipe consists of the following: 1) getting children to believe in themselves that they CAN do it; 2) getting their parents to understand that they are not lazy and to provide them with as much support and positive reinforcement; and 3) implementing an academic program that is specific to them and their needs so that they can succeed and make progress as quickly as possible

---

WATCH OUR *NEXT* INTERACTIVE ONLINE WEBINAR, FREE!

Sign up and you'll be invited to attend one of our upcoming Webinar events as a guest. You'll have a chance to "chat" with Noel live, ask questions, win prizes and meet other like-minded parents just like you that care about their children!

Visit www.BelieveAndGrowSmart.com **or text GROWSMART to 58885 or text your email address to (844) 906-0506**

---

11 STRATEGY 7: LETTER-WORD CONFIGURATION

"He that loves reading has everything within his reach."
William Godwin

Let's talk about the next strategy called letter-word configuration. We can use the color coding strategy and the chunking strategy in conjunction with letter-word configuration. The reason we would use this strategy is to help visual learners get a visual representation of the word by outlining it. Note: We use the color coding strategy and the chunking strategy so that we don't ignore principles of phonics and decoding. We want children to utilize as many ways to attack a word as possible. I also want you to recall that I don't believe in having children learn to read words using solely a visual strategy. The letter-word configuration strategy is just another way that children can learn words in a creative and fun way.

diversity

editor

effortlessly

eliminate

evidence

exaggerate

examine

familiar

favorable

federal

ferocious

festival

hemisphere

hesitate

historian

identify

illegible

imaginable

independent

indicate

industrial

informal

innocent

inspection

invincible

irregular

irritable

legislature

liberty

livelihood

miserable

misunderstood

moisture

numeral

numerous

nutritious

outnumbered

outstanding

parallel

peculiar

peppermint

performance

poverty

previous

primary

protective

reaction

reappear

represent

republic

residence

royalty

significant

skillfully

society

solution

summarize

superstitious

tambourine

unexpected

unfamiliar

unfortunately

utopia

various

CASE STUDY 10 (Initial Assessment)

Gender: female

Grade: 2.10 Retained

Age: 8 years, 5 months

Reading Test Results

Word Identification:	GE 2.4	AE 7-9
Reading Fluency:	GE 2.3	AE 7-7
Story Recall:	GE 1.7	AE 7-1
Understanding Directions:	GE 1.1	AE 6-5
Passage Comprehension:	GE 1.9	AE 7-2
Word Attack:	GE 3.1	AE 8-6
Oral Comprehension:	GE K.8	AE 6-1
Reading Vocabulary:	GE 1.6	AE 6-11
Sound Awareness:	GE 2.8	AE 8-5

I got a call from this student's older sister that wanted to get help for her little sister that was struggling to read. I asked her why she called me and not her mother. She told me that her mother didn't speak English that's why she made the initial contact. I invited her to bring her mother during the initial consultation since I speak Spanish. In addition, I asked her to bring in her sister's end of year report card and some work samples.

When I met with the mother and older sister during the initial consultation, the mother mentioned to me that her daughter was retained in second grade. The older sister helps her at home and sees that her younger sister is struggling to read. They told me that she did not like reading, that it was a battle to get her to read and when she did her homework often times it was wrong. They also told me that the previous summer, they enrolled her in a different program but did not see any improvement. They brought her in to get help at Connect the Dots Learning, because they had heard great things about the instruction and results that we delivered.

Let's talk about the results of the test. The area of strength for this student was her ability to attack words and utilize phonics and decoding skills. However, she needed support with words that contained multi-syllables, reading fluency, vocabulary and meaning and comprehension. She had just completed second grade and was still performing at about a low second grade level. I designed a program specifically tailored to her needs. The plan of attack was for her improve on strengthening her ability to attack words with multi-syllables, reading fluency and especially comprehension. I worked with her for 16 hours in a small group setting for a month. Below are the results of the post-assessment.

CASE STUDY 10 (Post-Assessment)

Gender: female

Grade: 2.10 Retained

Age: 8 years, 7 months

Reading Test Results

Word Identification:	GE 2.8	AE 8-1
Reading Fluency:	GE 2.7	AE 8-1

What is alliteration? Alliteration is when you have repetition of the same sounds at the beginning of words in a sentence. An example of alliteration that we are familiar with is Betty Botter by Mother Goose which reads: "Betty Botter bought some butter, but, she said, the butter's bitter; if I put it in my batter it will make my batter bitter, but a bit of better butter will make my batter better." We also see alliteration examples in tongue twisters such as this one which you may recognize: "Peter Piper picked a peck of pickled peppers. A peck of pickled peppers Peter Piper picked. If Peter Piper picked a peck of pickled peppers, how many pickled peppers did Peter Piper pick?" Another example of alliteration is in the names of businesses that are highly recognizable such as:

- Dunkin' Donuts
- PayPal
- Best Buy
- Coca-Cola
- Life Lock
- American Apparel
- American Airlines
- Chuck E Cheese's
- Bed Bath & Beyond
- Krispy Kreme

Here is an example of alliteration and how I would teach it. "Frank's five friends found four frogs on Friday". I will go ahead and read the sentence. Then I will invite the child to read the sentence with me. After that, I will have the child write the sentence on a piece of paper so that they can draw a picture. I will ask them, "What do you need to draw?" They will say, " I need to draw Frank." I will say, "who else or what else do you need to draw?" The child will say, "I also need to draw his five friends finding four frogs." I will say, "great! Do you need me to help you draw it or can you draw a picture by yourself?" They will either ask for help or do it on their own. Don't worry if art isn't one of your strong suits. Just do the best you can. They will enjoy this activity.

Once the child (or you) has finished drawing the picture, then you will ask them what each character is saying (including the frogs if you wish). Let them tell you what the characters are saying and write bubbles next to the characters inserting what your child says. Afterwards, let them color it. But make sure that they are able to read the sentence as well as what the characters are saying. We want them to have a mental picture of the alliteration sentence. In essence, we want them to visualize what the sentences says (which is wonderful for comprehension). A few examples of how you can use this strategy of drawing pictures in other ways includes having your child: draw the sequence of the story, the characters and the setting of a story, the plot of the story and the problem solved during the story. I really encourage you to let them draw and have fun. Let's take a look at our last case study.

CASE STUDY 11 (Initial Assessment)

Gender: female

Grade: K.10 Retained

Age: 6 years, 9 months

Reading Test Results

Word Identification:	GE <K.0	AE 4-2
Story Recall:	GE <K.0	AE 4-0
Understanding Directions:	GE K.2	AE 6-2
Passage Comprehension:	GE K.4	AE 5-6
Word Attack:	GE <K.0	AE <3-8

Oral Comprehension:	GE <K.0	AE 4-2
Reading Vocabulary:	GE <K.6	AE <5-10
Sound Awareness:	GE <K.0	AE 4-10

I got a call from this child's mother that was heavily concerned about her daughter. She told me that she was extremely far behind in reading. She mentioned that her daughter was in kindergarten so I wondered how far behind she could be. After all, it's only kindergarten. I asked her to bring in her daughter's end of year report card and some work samples.

When I met with the mother during the initial consultation, the mother mentioned to me that her daughter had been retained. I began to ask more questions because a child that is retained in kindergarten must need intensive support. The initial test results are above. I went on to see what letters of the alphabet she knew and she only knew 3 lowercase letters and 5 uppercase letters. After obtaining the test results I was certain that she needed to get academic support right away. In fact, I suspected that the child could possibly benefit from get tested to see if she qualified for Special Education services.

We've all heard that early intervention is key. In this case, early intervention was imperative. I wish that every story results in success. Unfortunately, I was not able to work with this child because the mother felt that the cost was too much. It saddens me because when I met the mother she was well manicured, well dressed and had her hair done as if she had recently gone to a salon. When I saw them leaving, I saw the vehicle that she drove and it was an expensive German car.

I understand that some families don't have the means to pay for private tutoring. I get that. But I just couldn't believe that the mother felt that the services were too costly considering that the vehicle she was driving was over $60,000. The questions that I had in my mind after she told me that it cost too much were: "How much is your child's education worth?" More importantly, how much is it worth for your child? What would it feel like to you, if your child started to improve in reading? More importantly, how would that feel like for your child? What would it feel like to you if your child started to gain her academic self-esteem? More importantly, how would that feel like for your child? What would it feel like to you if you saw your child make strides that you haven't seen? More importantly, how would that feel like for your child?"

I knew that my team and I at Connect the Dots Learning could help this child and get her on the right track but despite my best efforts we weren't able to help. I just hope that the mother has gotten her daughter the help that she desperately needs.

FINAL THOUGHTS

Congratulations, dear friend, you made it to the finish line! The preceding pages represent 18 years of hard work, experience and the efforts of my incredible team, students and the families I've served.

As you read throughout this book I shared with you many case studies that are just a small sample of the successes that my team and I have had at Connect the Dots Learning. What I need you do is to take action and get the help that your child needs now. Don't wait until they are so far behind that they begin to resent school, hate to read and lose their academic self-esteem. We live in an age where the academic environment is extremely rigorous. Unfortunately, children do get left behind, are promoted to the next grade level even though they may not have the academic skills to move on, and as a result suffer.

I also need you to be their best cheerleader. Children whether they are above, at, or below grade level need you to advocate for them and make sure that they are getting the best education possible. In the beginning of this book I asked you some questions which I will ask you again. If you could find a way to help your children build their academic self-confidence right now, this month, would you do it? How about improving their reading ability? Math ability? Writing ability? Maybe improving their reading, writing or math skills a grade level plus? I know that you would affirmatively answer yes! I know that you are committed to your child's education. I know that you will leverage my eighteen years of experience to help you so that your child has a better and brighter future. Lastly, I know that you will take full advantage of the many opportunities for you to go deeper in the content, gain access to several free training videos, participate in some interactive webinar events and register to get my up-to-date trainings because I want to help your children maximize their potential and add value to your life.

If you liked what you read, or most of what you read, I'd absolutely, positively love to hear from you and get to know you better and find out what you learned - or better yet, post a picture or video on the Connect the Dots Learning Facebook wall at www.Facebook.com/ConnectTheDotsLearning.

To your child's success!

To learn more about how to help your child improve over a grade level in reading, **visit** www.BelieveAndGrowSmart.com **or text GROWSMART to 58885 or text your email address to (844) 906-0506**